GROSS AND Frightening ANIMAL FACTS

DISGUSTING ANIMALS

Stella Tarakson

MASON CREST

THAT'S SICK!

Mason Crest
450 Parkway Drive, Suite D
Broomall, Pennsylvania 19008
(866) MCP-BOOK (toll free)

First printing
9 8 7 6 5 4 3 2 1

ISBN (hardback) 978-1-4222-3925-4
ISBN (series) 978-1-4222-3923-0
ISBN (ebook) 978-1-4222-7862-8

Cataloging-in-Publication Data on file with the Library of Congress

Disgusting Animals
Text copyright © 2015 Pascal Press Written by Stella Tarakson

First published 2015 by Pascal Press PO Box 250, Glebe, NSW 2037 Australia

Publisher: Lynn Dickinson Principal Photographer: Steve Parish © Nature-Connect Pty Ltd
Additional Photography: See p. 48 Researcher: Clare Thomson, Wild Card Media Editor: Vanessa Barker

CONTENTS

THAT'S SICK!

CHAPTER 1

DISGUSTING DIETS

Bats, rats, intestines and blood—we might find eating such things weird, but in many parts of the world, it's completely natural!

A GUTFUL

If you've ever been to Scotland, you might have tried haggis. It's a savory pudding containing sheep's heart, liver and lungs, minced up with onion, oatmeal and suet. The filling is encased in the animal's stomach and slowly simmered.

I'M TASTIER THAN YOU THINK!

VAMPIRE'S DELIGHT

What would you eat for breakfast at Dracula's castle? Blood pudding, of course! Also called blood sausage or black pudding, this claret-colored sausage is made of oatmeal and the main ingredient — congealed pig's blood!

SLOW FOOD

Escargot means "snail" in French, and this slimy mollusc is actually considered a delicacy in France. The snails first have to be purged for several days to poop out any toxins in their bodies that could be poisonous to humans. The snails are then boiled, scooped from their shells, fried in butter and garlic, and then placed back into their shells before serving. Bon appetit!

NEEDS MORE GARLIC!

ROASTED RODENT

Forget the stir-fry—try some rat meat when you're next in Asia! Or maybe you'd prefer smoked bat, another popular meat in the region. If you're a fan of seafood, head over to Korea to try some live octopus. Just watch out that the slippery suckers don't stick to your tongue!

EATING BUGS

We might feel queasy at the thought of eating scuttling spiders and insects, but more than 2.5 billion people would disagree. People in more than 100 countries eat bugs—1,500 different types! Bugs are a good source of protein and fat and could well help solve the problem of worldwide famine. So keep an open mind!

YUCK! THERE'S A HUMAN IN MY SOUP!

TUCK IN

Many Aboriginal bush tucker foods like witchetty grubs, termites and praying mantis do double duty as medicines. Aboriginal peoples in some parts of central Australia crush witchetty grubs into a paste and use it to soothe burns.

BUGS GALORE

Next time you travel overseas, seek out these local treats. Join the Chinese in eating maggots, cicadas and scorpions. The Japanese prefer wasp pupae and bamboo caterpillars. Thailand is famous for its silk, but did you know that people there also eat silkworm pupae? Maybe you could try munching on mole crickets in the Philippines or slurping down sago palm weevil grubs in Indonesia. The truly brave can even try tarantulas in Cambodia and Venezuela!

SUCK OUT THEIR BRAINS!

Giant water bugs are a snack in Thailand.

Fried cicada

Ancient Treats

Bugs have been on the menu for many years. Fossil bone tools found in South Africa suggest that our ancient relatives, previously thought to be vegetarian, may have been digging in termite mounds for their dinner. These early entomologists may not have realized it, but they were getting a delicious and nutritious snack full of protein and fat!

BEST SELLER

Fancy an earthworm omelette, honeybee soufflé or insect quiche? Why not add a book on insect cookery to your Christmas wish list? There are more out there than you'd think!

SPREAD OUT THE GOODNESS

Here's a 19th-century recipe for cockroach pâté: "Made from cockroaches simmered in vinegar all morning and then dried in the sun . . . then boiled with butter, farina, pepper and salt to make a paste which is spread on buttered bread."

DOUBLE HOPPER MEAL

Did you know that many insects are richer in minerals than meats such as hamburger? A gram of crickets or grasshoppers can be more nutritious than an equal amount of beef or pork! An average hamburger contains 0.5 ounces (15 grams) of fat and 0.8 ounces (22 grams) of protein. An equivalent serving of crickets has about the same levels of protein but just 0.2 ounces (6 grams) of fat. Hop to it!

WANTED FARMHANDS

Cockroach farming is becoming big business in China, where there are around 100 cockroach farms. That's tens of millions of crunchy critters being bred to make pulverized cockroach powder that is used in medicines and cosmetics.

Has anyone ever called you garbage guts? Maybe when you wolfed down that burger too quickly? Don't worry, that's nothing compared to some animals who eat almost anything—and not all of it is food! Police shot a rogue crocodile and found some amazing things in its stomach: a pair of shorts, a football and a diaper!

DON'T THROW THAT AWAY, IT'S PERFECTLY GOOD!

GARBAGE GUTS

YUMMY!

WHAT A LOAD OF RUBBISH

A diamond python found had a tea towel, two lengths of cord, cellophane wrapping and pieces of paper in its stomach.

I'M JUST TAKING OUT THE GARBAGE!

WHALE OF A DIET

Some whales just eat krill, but killer whales eat almost anything they can catch. This can include dolphins, seals, fish, turtles, squid, birds—even other whales! A killer whale was even found with the remains of 13 porpoises and 14 seals in its stomach.

DON'T GULP YOUR FOOD

Think of this the next time your mom tells you to chew your food properly. A 15-foot (4.6-meter)-long great white shark caught in New Zealand was found to have a whole bull seal in her stomach! The seal weighed 160–180 pounds (80–90 kilograms) and had been eaten in just two pieces. CRUNCH CRUNCH!

I'VE GOT TERRIBLE INDIGESTION!

KILLER PLASTIC

The greatest threat to marine life isn't a predator—it's plastic! Every year, more than 520 billion pounds (236 million tonnes) of the plastic we use ends up in the world's oceans. Unlike more natural materials, plastic doesn't break down completely. Tragically, seabirds often mistake colorful bits of plastic for sea life. They eat it or feed it to their chicks. Many others become entangled or choked. Around the world, about 1 million seabirds and 100,000 marine mammals are killed every year by plastics.

In the year 2000, a deceased 26-foot (8- meter)-long bryde's whale was found in Queensland. Its stomach was packed with 65 square feet (6 square meters) of plastic.

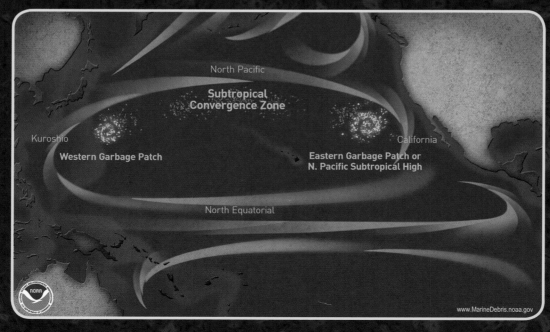

North Pacific

Subtropical Convergence Zone

Kuroshio

Western Garbage Patch

California

Eastern Garbage Patch or N. Pacific Subtropical High

North Equatorial

www.MarineDebris.noaa.gov

Marine debris accumulation locations in the North Pacific Ocean

This albatross chick was accidentally fed plastic by its parents. It died as a result. You can see a pen in the remains of its stomach.

ANCIENT VOMIT

Jurassic puke has been discovered near an English town, much to the delight of paleontologists! Copious quantities of fossilized vomit dating back 160 million years were unearthed in a clay quarry. The culprit? Researchers believe the super-puker was an ichthyosaur, an ancient marine reptile that ate squid-like shellfish called belemnites. The shells showed signs of being attacked by the dinosaur's stomach juices.

RAPID RESPONSE VOMIT

Have you ever felt so frightened that you could vomit? Hopefully not! Baby Eurasian rollers are the experts, however. When they feel threatened, the birds vomit a foul-smelling liquid onto themselves. The smelly, orange liquid puts off predators and lets the parents know they need help.

THE INSIDE-OUT FROG

If frogs eat something poisonous or yucky, they can turn their stomachs completely inside out! They wipe away any gunk with their feet then swallow their stomach back in. Wouldn't that be a great party trick!

YOU DON'T WANT ME WHEN I'M COVERED WITH PUKE!

MAYBE THEY CAN BOTTLE MY FARTS?

WHAT'S THAT SMELL?

How would you like to earn lots of money by combing the beach—for whale waste! Ambergris is a solid, waxy material produced by a sperm whale's digestive system. If a sperm whale swallows something sharp—like the beak of a giant squid—it might vomit it up. If it can't manage that, the sharp object will get covered in a waxy substance called ambergris, which protects the whale's digestive system. At first ambergris is unpleasantly smelly, but over time it mellows to something less objectionable. In fact, ambergris is highly valued in the perfume industry!

AFTER SPRAYING PERFUME, JENNY ALWAYS SAW MORE WHALES...

ACID BATH

Carrion-eating vultures take the defensive-puking strategy one step further. Their vomit smells so badly, just a sniff of it can drive away predators. Woe to those who ignore the smell and get too close as the acid-laden vomit is strong enough to burn!

SICK TACTICS

PURE SICK!

You've heard of animals that defend themselves with stings and venom, but did you know that some chase off their enemies with spew? The caterpillars of the large, white butterfly protect themselves by vomiting on their predators. Who'd believe that they turn into such pretty butterflies!

Shearwaters might look cute, but they have a sickening defense mechanism. When threatened, they spit out a stinky stream of stomach oil!

SHEAR SICKNESS

BLAH!

I'VE NEVER THROWN UP!

WHERE'S MY CLAY?

Did you know that rats and mice don't throw up? Most mammals have a vomiting reflex to protect them from ingesting harmful substances. But when rodents feel sick, they eat clay. Substances in the clay can latch onto dangerous materials, preventing them from being absorbed.

Four people had to go to the hospital after breathing in the fumes of a dog's vomit. The dog had eaten rat poison!

YOU'VE GOT IT LICKED

THIS TASTES LIKE A PILE OF RABBIT POO!

Your tongue can detect five separate tastes: sweet, salty, sour, bitter and umami (pleasant savory). But what about all those other flavors? They come mainly through our sense of smell, which is why food tastes bland when you have a cold. People used to believe different tastes were sensed on different parts of the tongue—they even created a "tongue map"! Now we know that every taste bud detects every taste. A taste bud is a collection of sensory cells. They're found in the thousands of tiny bumps on your tongue called papillae. Without taste buds, it would be harder to determine whether something is good and safe to eat.

NOSE-LICKING GOOD

YOU TRY PICKING YOUR NOSE WITH HOOVES!

Imagine if you could clean out your nostrils with your tongue? Cows can!

What would a kangaro or wallaby do without its tongue?

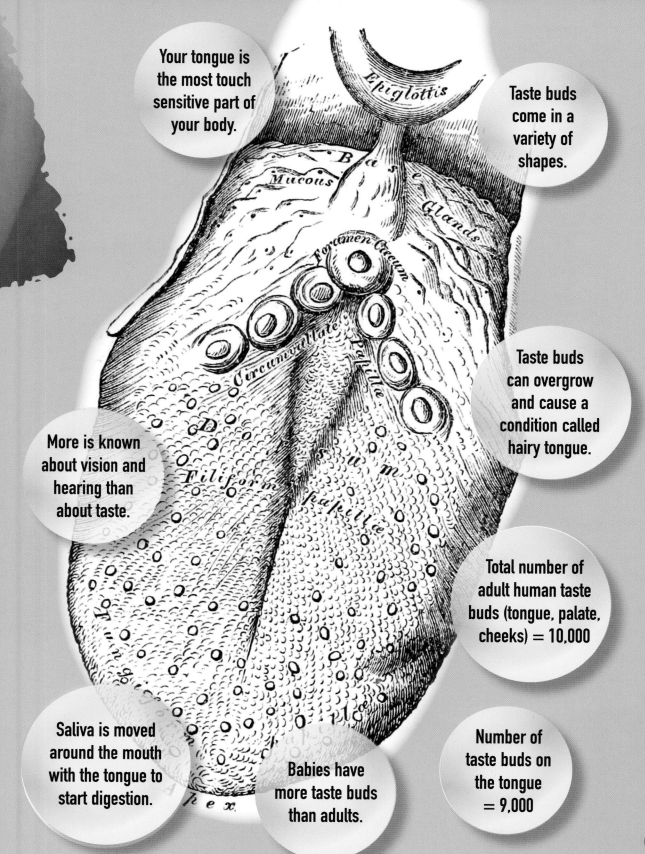

Your tongue is the most touch sensitive part of your body.

Taste buds come in a variety of shapes.

Taste buds can overgrow and cause a condition called hairy tongue.

More is known about vision and hearing than about taste.

Total number of adult human taste buds (tongue, palate, cheeks) = 10,000

Saliva is moved around the mouth with the tongue to start digestion.

Babies have more taste buds than adults.

Number of taste buds on the tongue = 9,000

SICK TONGUES

THIS IS A NO-FLY ZONE!

STICKY LICKY

An echidna has no teeth—but it more than makes up for it with its incredible tongue. At up to 7 inches (18 centimeters) long, an echidna's tongue is nearly half the length of its body! The tongue is covered in saliva to quickly start digesting the ants it licks up.

TOP GUN TONGUE

It only takes a chameleon 0.07 of a second to unfurl its tongue, which is twice the length of its body! Scientists took high-speed films of chameleons catching prey. They showed that the tip of the chameleon's tongue accelerates with five times the acceleration of a fighter jet! It doesn't leave insects with much time to escape...

tongue poke

We know we shouldn't do it, but it's tempting when someone annoys us! Skinks poke out their tongues, too, but far more impressively. If provoked or threatened, blue-tongued and pink-tongued skinks turn to face their aggressors. With mouths open wide, they poke out their brightly colored tongues, all while hissing and puffing up their bodies. Although it's mostly bluff, don't return the signal. Skinks have strong jaws, and their bite is painful!

GET READY

SCARY

CHAPTER 2

SICK DESIGNS

From spitting on food to sleeping in snot, animals have found some unique (but sick) ways to survive the challenges of life. Warning—don't try these at home!

SALIVA SOUP

Scorpions have the worst table manners! They catch their prey in their massive claws—then tear it up and dribble saliva all over it! The saliva starts off the digestion process. Once the food is suitably mushy, the scorpions suck it up like soup.

SEWER DWELLERS

THIS TASTES LIKE POO!

IT IS POO!

Cockroaches live in the most disgusting places, including sewers and toilets. They'll eat anything, even pus, spit and decaying rubbish! But cockroaches need to keep themselves clean through grooming—like wiping their antennae obsessively—otherwise they lose their sense of smell. Cockroaches are filled with bacteria as well as white fatty pus—which squelches out if you stomp on them!

MUCUS SLEEPING BAGS

Some parrotfish make sleeping bags out of slime! They use mucus from glands in their heads to create these bags before they settle down for the night. The sleeping bag is designed to protect the fish from sharks and moray eels. In the morning, the parrotfish swims out of the bag in search of breakfast.

CHAPTER 3

SICK HABITS

Nose picking, bottom scratching, burping—some people have all sorts of bad habits, and they're not alone! Animals have some pretty sick habits too—even ones that'll make your brother look like an angel!

Impressive!

Unimpressive!

FOAMING AT THE MOUTH

Male dromedary camels have a sick trick to impress the chicks. They inflate their tongue like a limp balloon and hang it out the side of their mouths! It's called the dhula and droops down 10–14 inches (25–35 centimeters). The male tops off his display with a mass of foamy saliva, tossing his head up and down. The dhula flops around, and slobbery spit sprays all over the place!

THE DEAD SKIN DIET

Do you find paper, books, works of art and nylon stockings tasty? Silverfish do! They also can't get enough of the taste of flaked-off human skin. Still, we have to give these eccentric eaters some credit. Silverfish are living fossils and the closest thing there is to the first insects that ever lived.

A POUND (HALF KILO) OF FROG MEAT PLEASES!

Butcherbirds got their names for a good reason. Like a butcher in a shop, they hang up their prey on hooks or tree forks. And they whistle just as cheerfully, too! Butcherbirds prey on small animals like frogs, reptiles, birds and insects. They swoop onto their prey, which is usually on the ground.

CHAPTER 4

MOTHER KNOWS BEST

Our moms have said it countless times, but these little critters probably wouldn't want to argue!

MOM THE BUILDER

Some moms go to great lengths to provide for their young. Various species of wasps, such as the spider wasp and the mud-dauber wasp, make sure their babies have something tasty to eat even before they hatch! The wasps paralyze spiders with their stings and drag them to their nests, which are made up of individual chambers formed from mud or clay. One or more spiders are placed in each chamber, and a wasp egg is laid in or on the spiders. When the wasp larva hatches, it eats the paralyzed spiders and pupates before emerging from the chamber as a fully formed wasp.

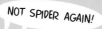

NOT SPIDER AGAIN!

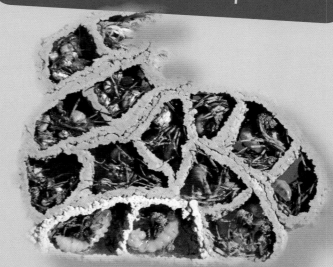

ALL ABOARD!

PUBLIC TRANSPORT

Baby wolf spiders get a free ride for up to seven months. After hatching, the hundreds of tiny spiders arrange themselves in neat rows on their mother's back and stay there until they can fend for themselves. No pushing, please!

DIGESTIBLE DAD

The red-back spider female is much larger than the male—the size of a marble compared to a single grain of rice. When they mate, the female sticks her fangs into the male and digests him. This is so her babies have an extra meal. But Dad's so small, he's more of an appetizer than a main course!

Parasites are some of the most plentiful and adaptable species on Earth. There are around 6.8 million of them—that's four parasites for each of the estimated 1.7 million different species on our planet! They can also make their homes almost anywhere in the body—including the brain, bladder and tongue—and can eat almost anything. Anyone for a blood, guts and snot shake?

WORM
INFESTATION

Ever suffered from the dreaded bottom itch? Most likely it was caused by threadworms, tiny white parasites that look like bits of thread. Threadworms come out of the anus at night to lay their eggs. They're spread by children scratching their bottoms and carrying the worm eggs back to their mouths with their fingers. Another very good reason to wash your hands!

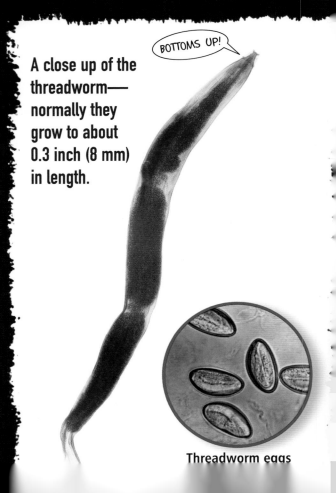

BOTTOMS UP!

A close up of the threadworm—normally they grow to about 0.3 inch (8 mm) in length.

Threadworm eggs

TERRIBLE TAPEWORMS

Tapeworms can infest humans and set up residence in their intestines. They can increase their size by 1.8 million times in just two weeks and can stretch like ribbons for up to 62 feet (18 meters)! People get them by ingesting tapeworm eggs or larvae, usually from infected food or water. Untreated, tapeworms can live in a body for up to 20 years!

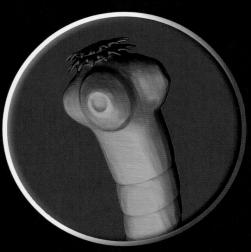

The worm's head is called the scolex. The scolex has suckers or hooks that attach to the intestinal wall of its host.

MOSQUITO INVASION

Mosquitoes have caused more deaths than any other animal in the world! They're responsible for the transmission of many serious diseases, including malaria. There are more than 300 different species of mosquito within Australia alone!

PARASITE INJECTION

BURP!

Are you scared of needles? Well, this is one injection you definitely won't want to get. Malaria is caused by the world's most lethal parasite. It is spread by mosquitoes that "inject" the parasite into the human body. The parasite infests the liver and then the red blood cells, which eventually burst.

Female mosquitoes have elastic-sided bodies that allow them to drink up to four times their weight in blood. More blood equals more eggs, so reproduction is thirsty work!

RIVERS OF SWEAT

Mosquitoes also transmit Ross River Fever, which is caused by a virus. Ross River Fever is common throughout Australia, particularly along the coast and around inland waters. Epidemics can occur during heavy rainfalls, floods and high temperatures—conditions that mosquitoes love!

magnified virus

Did you know the word "virus" comes from the Latin word for poison or slimy liquid? Viruses can't reproduce on their own and can only replicate by infecting a host cell. Some viruses reproduce so aggressively that they end up killing their host!

ZOMBIE PARASITES

Watch out for zombie-making parasites! No, it's not something from a movie—it's real. Some parasites take over the nervous systems of their hosts and force them to their will. Spiders in Costa Rica build webs for parasitic wasps living inside them, while horsehair worms force land-dwelling hosts like grasshoppers to enter water. What's the reason for their mind-bending powers? It's the spread of their species, of course, and … eventually … to take over the world!

This horsehair worm forced its bush-cricket host to drown itself in a puddle.

A horsehair worm emerges from the abdomen of its host.

SLIME BALLS AND ZOMBIE VOODOO

How do lancet flukes do the voodoo? They infest the ant's nervous system, allowing them to control its movements. At night, they make the ant climb up a tall blade of grass and stay there, sitting and waiting to be eaten by a cow! If the ant doesn't get eaten overnight, it retreats back down the stalk to avoid the parasite-destroying sunlight. The cycle continues until the ant is eventually eaten.

The cow eats the ant, which infects the cow with lancet flukes.

The fluke lives in the cow's liver. Its eggs end up in the cow's poo.

An ant comes along and swallows the infested slime balls.

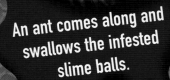

A snail eats the eggs, and the fluke hatches. The parasite makes the snail produce fluke-filled slime balls.

IS THAT REALLY YOUR TONGUE?

When is a tongue not a tongue? When it's a parasite! The tongue-eating louse enters through a fish's gills and hooks onto its tongue with its strong legs. The parasite cuts off the blood supply to the fish's tongue, causing it to wither away. There the parasite stays, living its happy life as an artificial tongue!

The underside of the tongue-eating louse shows an array of nasty hooks.

I WAS HOOKED ON YOU!

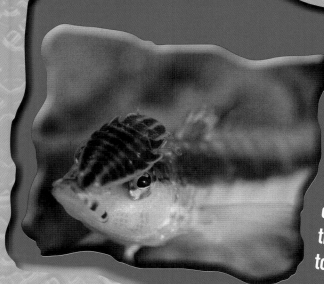

WON'T LET GO

The tongue-eating louse is a type of crustacean known as an isopod. It belongs to the cymothoidae family, a group of fish parasites. The parasites can latch onto the fish's mouth, gills or fins. Some types even burrow into the fish's flesh! This isopod is attached to the top of a lizardfish.

FREE RIDE

A close-up photo of a southern right whale reveals loads of lice feeding on the whale's dead skin. The lice are transferred between whales through bodily contact.

DON'T LET THE BED BUGS BITE

Bed bugs aren't something most Australians are familiar with—but that's about to change. It seems these irritating critters love hopping into travelers' suitcases and hitching a ride Down Under. So much so, that since 1999 there's been a 5000 percent increase in the number of bed bug infestations in the country! Bed bugs hide during the day, but at night they pierce the skin of sleeping people and suck their blood. The saliva they inject during feeding has anticoagulant properties, which means it stops the blood from clotting. While we're their favorite hosts, they occasionally snack on other warm-blooded animals.

Your favorite pillow might be home to many sickening bugs and potentially deadly fungi. The typical pillow contains more than one million fungal spores! They also harbor dust mites—microscopic eight-legged creatures that feed on flakes of human skin. The mites eat the fungi and the fungi eat dust mite poo. Fancy a midnight snack?

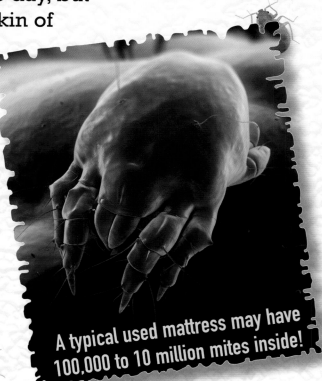

A typical used mattress may have 100,000 to 10 million mites inside!

EATEN INSIDE OUT

Most people are scared of a wasp's powerful sting, but getting stung is much more frightening for the caterpillar of a butterfly or moth! There are more than 12,000 species of wasps in Australia, some of which are parasitic. Found in urban areas, forests, woodlands and wetlands across the country, these flying assassins use their long ovipositors to inject their eggs inside or on their victims. The host usually stays alive until the wasp larvae hatch and proceed to eat it—killing it slowly, sometimes from the inside out. That's one deadly dinner party you definitely wouldn't want to be invited to!

BOTTOM-BREATHING BABIES

Maggots may look disgusting, but when you learn more about them, you discover that they really ARE disgusting! Maggots are the larvae of houseflies and have no eyes, legs or antennae. Instead, they have hooks on their heads that enable them to move around. They even breathe through two holes in their bottoms! Maggots break out of their larval case by filling their heads with fluid and bashing against the case until it cracks.

MY BABIES!

Maggots can be applied to wounds to consume infected tissue.

I CAN STILL BE A FUN GIRL!

FUNGAL FLY TRAP

Insects can be parasites—but they have their own problems too. Houseflies can become victims to a parasitic fungus, which infects and kills them. Flies are infected if struck by spores. The infected fly is forced to land, while the fungus grows in its abdomen, which swells up. Male flies are attracted to the swollen female flies and try to mate with them. The fungus eats the fly's insides and then breaks out to spread its spores even further.

LEECHES

I'M GETTING QUITE ATTACHED TO YOU!

Ever heard the expression "leeching off" someone? It means to take advantage of them without giving anything back. And that's just what leeches do! They clamp themselves onto hosts and suck their blood. Leeches can ingest several times their own weight in blood in one meal. After feeding, the leech unlatches and digests its meal. Digestion is slow, and the leech can last several months without food.

GET OFF!

Leeches inject a chemical that stops blood from clotting, so care must be taken if you try to remove one. The easiest way to get rid of a leech is to just let it finish its meal. It will drop off painlessly by itself, sealing off the wound. A hungry leech will only drink a couple of teaspoons (10 milliliters) of blood.

DR. LEECH

Leeches have been used as a medical treatment for thousands of years. The idea was that certain illnesses were caused by "bad blood," and leeches could remove some of that blood. Developments in medicine saw the end of such beliefs. But now leeches are wriggling their way back into modern medicine! They're being used in microsurgery—for instance, when fingers are reattached and there's a buildup of blood. Leeches are also being used to treat varicose veins ... but maybe you shouldn't tell Gran!

INSIDE A LEECH

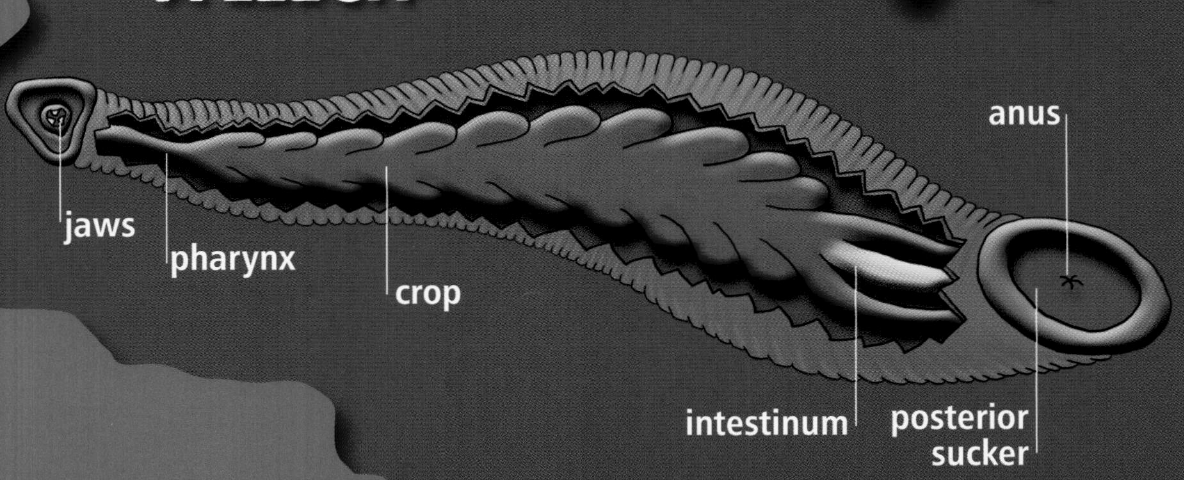

jaws

pharynx

crop

intestinum

posterior sucker

anus

TICKS

Everyone loves ticks—but only when adding up a winning score! Ticks can spread illnesses, such as Lyme Disease. Ticks aren't actually insects. Like spiders, they are eight-legged arachnids with two body segments. Six-legged insects have three body segments. Ticks are usually found outdoors in grassy or forested areas. There are many different types of ticks. The paralysis tick is a particular threat to dogs and other domestic animals.

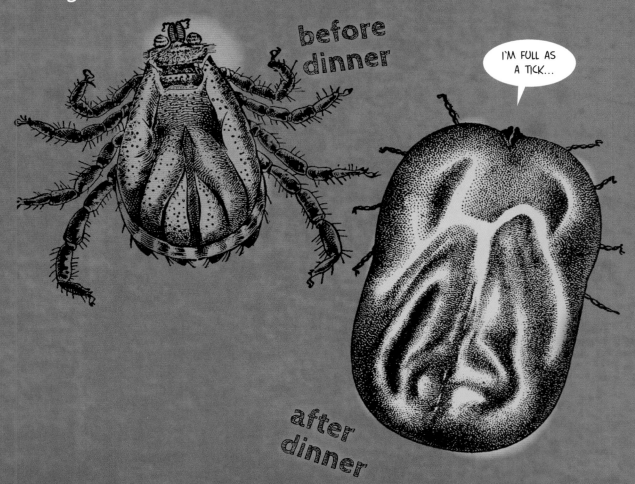

before dinner

I'M FULL AS A TICK...

after dinner

TICKING TIME BOMB

Ever wondered how ticks find their hosts? They have special organs on the fronts of their legs. These organs can detect body heat, pheromones (a type of chemical odor) and the carbon dioxide that animals breathe out. Ticks climb up the nearest plant to lie in wait. They latch onto anything that comes close—including your legs!

I SAW YOU

A tick's mouthparts act like little saws that cut into the skin. Once they've dug in, the tick can hang on for up to a week getting its fill!

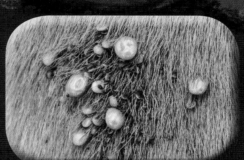

A dog with ticks in various stages of feeding.

GET A GRIP

Ticks have special mouthparts with feelers, pincers and a needle-like probe through which they suck blood. The probe has curved hooks that act like anchors—making the tick hard to remove.

FLEAS

Fleas are very small, but if you look at one under a microscope, you'd see that the little bloodsucker has two sets of tubes. One tube is used to suck blood into the flea's throat, while the other sends saliva down onto the host's skin. No wonder they make us itch! The flea's scientific name is siphonaptera. It sounds a bit like a dinosaur name, but it actually means "wingless siphon."

Fleas may be small now, but they used to be much bigger. About 165 million years ago, they were 0.8 inches (2 cm) long and fed off dinosaurs!

LITTLE BLEEDERS

Female fleas can consume 15 times their own body weight in blood daily. Adult fleas need a blood meal in order to lay eggs and to survive but can live up to 12 months without feeding. That's a long time between lunch and dinner!

RUN AND FLEA

SEE YOU LATER!

How are you at the long jump? Bet you can't beat a flea! A flea can cover 12 inches (30 entimeters) in a single leap. It doesn't sound like much, but it's nearly 125 times the length of its body. To do the equivalent, we'd have to jump over two-and-a-half football fields! Special bands above the flea's hind legs work like rubber bands. They store energy when stretched—then release it with a snap that flings the flea through the air.

FLEA CIRCUS

People used to flock to watch flea acrobats pulling miniature chariots and carriages. The fleas danced, juggled, played musical instruments and even turned a Ferris wheel! It all looked amazing, but the fleas weren't really trained. They were harnessed or glued to the props. What looked like polished performances were actually their attempts to break free!

THAT'S SICK!

GLOSSARY

adaptable	when something is able to change so that it becomes suited to a different situation
anus	the body opening that waste material from the bowel comes out of
carrion	the rotting flesh of dead animals out in the wild
congealed	when liquid thickens and becomes solid
deceased	when something has died
delicacy	an expensive or tasty food
digest	when food is eaten and then broken down by the stomach and intestines to be used by the body
entomologist	a person who studies insects
epidemic	when many people become sick from an illness in a short period of time
famine	an extreme shortage of food often caused by drought
farina	flour made from cereal grains and used in puddings or cooked as cereal
infestation	when a place is invaded or overrun by a pest in very large numbers
inflate	to fill something up with air or gas so it is firmer and larger
intestine	a long tube that carries food from the stomach to the anus

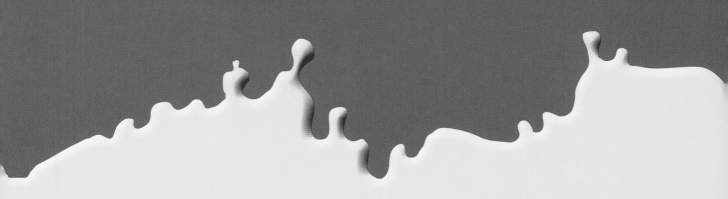

nervous system	the system of the body that includes the brain and nerve fibers, giving the body the ability to feel and move
paleontologist	a person who studies forms of life from very long ago, such as fossilized animals and plants
paralysis	the inability to move due to the muscles not working properly
parasite	a plant or animal that lives in or on another plant or animal and then feeds on it
pulverized	when something has been ground down into a dust or powder
reflex	an action that is done without thinking and is a reaction to something
spore	a reproductive cell produced by some plants
suet	a hard, fatty tissue from cattle and sheep that is used for cooking
transmission	when something is passed on to another person or place
unfurl	to unfold something and spread it out or shake it
varicose vein	a vein that is unusually large and swollen
wither	to dry up and shrink
wound	an injury, such as a cut or burn, made to living tissue

Additional images:

Richard Bartz: p. 43 (close-up of tick) *Chelicerae of a sheep tick*/CC BY-SA 2.5, http://commons.wikimedia.org/wiki/File:Ixodus_ricinus_5x.jpg; H.V. Carter: p. 19 (tongue) *Upper surface of the tongue* (Fig. 275) from *Anatomy: descriptive and surgical* 1st ed., by Henry Gray, 1858, London: J.W. Parker; John T. Creighton: p. 45 (flea) *Adult human flea* from *Household Pests*, 1943, Gainesville: Agricultural Extension Service; Alvin Davison: p. 42 (ticks) *Cattle tick* from *Practical Zoology*, 1906, New York: American Book Company; DPDx/PHI: p. 28 (threadworm eggs); J.G. Francis: p. 45 (flea circus illustrations) from 'The smallest circus in the world' by C.F. Holder. *St. Nicholas an Illustrated Magazine for Young Folks,* Part II, Volume XIII, May 1886 to October 1886, New York, New York: The Century Co.; Greg Harm: p. 8 (earthworms); Hans Hillewaert: p. 39 (fly with fungus) *Fly fungus on Common yellow dung fly at Oostende, Belgium*/© Hans Hillewaert/CC-BY-SA-4.0, http://commons.wikimedia.org/wiki/File:Entomophthora_muscae_on_Scathophaga_stercoraria_(lateral_view).jpg; Peter Kaminski: p. 15 (ambergris) *Whale ambergris*/CC BY 2.0, http://www.flickr.com/photos/peterkaminski/128588176/; Lukeosborne: p. 26 (spider wasp nest) *Lukeosborne* p. 32 (horsehair worm emerging from bush-cricket abdomen) *Nematomorpha*/CC BY-SA 2.0, https://www.flickr.com/photos/sanmartin/7973589340; Ian Morris: p. 6 (witchetty grubs); NOAA: p. 12 (marine debris map) *Marine debris accumulation locations in the North Pacific Ocean*, http://commons.wikimedia.org/wiki/File:Pacific-garbage-patch-map_2010_noaamdp.jpg; T. Jeffrey Parker: p. 40 (medical leech) *Head of Hirudo medicinalis* (Fig. 118a) from *A Manual of Zoology*, 1900, New York, NY: The MacMillan Company; Alastair Rae: p. 32 (horsehair worm and cricket) *Horsehair worm*/CC BY-SA 2.0, https://www.flickr.com/photos/merula/14629048952; Joseph Schäk: p. 29 (tapeworm) from *Drittes Lesebuch*, 1874, New York: Fr. Pustet; Ken Stepnell: pp. 10 (diamond python) & 27 (red-back spider); Valerie Taylor: pp. 11 (great white shark), 15 (sperm whale calf) & 35 (lice on southern right whale); Marco Vinci: p. 34 (underside of tongue-eating louse) *Cymothoa exigua*/CC BY-SA 3.0, http://commons.wikimedia.org/wiki/File:Cymothoa_exigua_(capovolta).JPG; Duncan Wright/USFWS: p. 13 (albatross chick remains), http://commons.wikimedia.org/wiki/File:Albatross_chick_plastic.jpg.

Licences:

http://creativecommons.org/publicdomain/zero/1.0/deed.en
http://creativecommons.org/licenses/by/2.0/
http://creativecommons.org/licenses/by-sa/2.0/
http://creativecommons.org/licenses/by-sa/2.5/deed.en
http://creativecommons.org/licenses/by-sa/3.0/deed.en
http://creativecommons.org/licenses/by-sa/4.0/deed.en